This book belongs to:

Abby Lowe

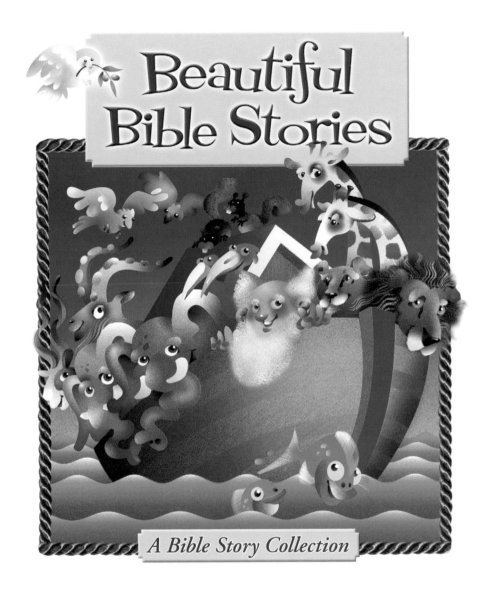

Beautiful Bible Stories

A Bible Story Collection

Illustrated by Cheryl Mendenhall

Beautiful Bible Stories

GOD'S CREATION

Adapted by Tess Fries

Long, long ago the world was very different than it is now. In fact, the world did not exist at all! There was only dark, empty space. But God was in the darkness, and He had a plan to make something good.

God created the heavens and the earth, and the earth was covered with water.

God said, "Let there be light," and a golden light shone everywhere. He called the light day and the dark night. This was the very first day.

On the second day, God made the beautiful blue sky with clouds to hold the raindrops.

On the third day, God separated the sparkling waters from the land and formed the seas and rivers.

He shaped the great mountains and the sloping valleys from the land, then sprinkled the deserts with sand. He planted the fields with tall grasses, trees and colorful flowers. At the end of the third day, God saw that it was good.

God put lights in the heavens on the fourth day. He made the brilliant sun for the daytime and the gentle light of the moon for the night. He placed each star in just the right spot and made them twinkle and shine.

On the fifth day, God made the gigantic whales and the slithering eels. He made the sharks and octopus and every kind of fish to fill the waters.

God also made the birds to sail on the wind and fly through the sky. He made the mighty eagles, the honking geese and the tiny hummingbirds.

On the sixth day, God made all of the animals. He made some with antlers and some with pouches. He created animals that galloped, hopped, roared, growled and mooed.

God wanted someone to rule over the earth and to enjoy His creation. So on the sixth day, God also made the first man. He made him from the dust of the earth and breathed into him the breath of life. God named him Adam.

On the seventh day, God rested. He saw everything He had made, and He knew that it was good.

God is the maker of all things. There will never be anyone greater or more powerful than God.

God made you just the way you are. He wants you to enjoy His creations and to love Him, for He knows that this is good.

*God saw all that he had made,
and it was very good.*

—Genesis 1:31

ADAM & EVE

Adapted by Tess Fries

Long ago, when God made the world and all that was in it, He created the very first man. The man's name was Adam. God made Adam from the dust of the ground, and then He breathed life into him.

God put Adam in a wonderful place called the Garden of Eden. There were all kinds of plants, animals and trees in the garden. The trees were beautiful. Some trees had wonderful fruit that Adam could eat and enjoy.

In the middle of the garden grew the Tree of Knowledge of Good and Evil.

God told Adam, "You may eat the fruit from every tree in the garden except the Tree of Knowledge of Good and Evil. The day that you eat from that tree —you will die."

Adam spent time in the garden tending the plants for God. It was joyful work and a happy life for Adam.

One day, God brought all the marvelous creatures He had made to Adam and gave him the job of naming them. Adam named the rhinos, the frogs, the raven and the lions. Large and small, furry and feathered, Adam gave each one a name.

After all of the animals were named, God looked at Adam and said, "It is not good for man to be alone." He caused Adam to fall into a very deep sleep. God then took one of Adam's ribs and from it made the first woman. Her name was Eve and she became Adam's wife.

They enjoyed living in the garden among the friendly animals and the beautiful plants. But the best part was being near God, and walking and talking with Him in the garden.

Now, the serpent was a very deceptive creature in the garden. One day he came to Eve and said, "You will not die if you eat the fruit from the Tree of Knowledge of Good and Evil. God knows that if you eat it, you will become a god like He is."

Eve looked at the fruit. It was beautiful and looked like it would taste delicious. Eve decided to believe the serpent instead of listening to God. She took the fruit and ate it. She gave some to Adam— and he ate it, too.

At once, Adam and Eve knew they had done something terribly wrong! They had disobeyed God. They were ashamed and afraid.

Later, they heard God's voice as He walked through the garden, so they hid. "Adam, where are you?" God asked. Adam said, "I heard Your voice, and I was afraid." God asked Adam if he had eaten the forbidden fruit. Adam replied, "Eve gave me the fruit, and I ate it."

God was not happy that Adam and Eve had disobeyed Him and were deceived by the serpent. He said to the serpent, "Because of this, you will have to crawl on your belly forever."

Then God told Adam and Eve, "Because you have eaten the forbidden fruit, you must leave the garden," and He drove them out of the Garden of Eden.

Cherubim were placed at the entrance of the garden to guard it.

Adam and Eve began their new lives outside the garden. They had to make a home among the rocks and trees. They worked hard to grow food among the thistles and weeds. But worst of all, they could no longer walk with God.

Because they had disobeyed God, Adam and Eve—and everyone born after them—would die as God had said. But God's love is so great, He sent His Son to take the punishment for all our sins, so that we can have eternal life.

The LORD *God took the man*
and put him in the Garden of Eden
to work it and take care of it.

—Genesis 2:15

Noah's Ark

Adapted by Shawn South Aswad

Long, long ago there lived a very special man whose name was Noah. Noah was special because God chose him to do an important job.

One day, God said to Noah, "I am not happy with the people on earth and have decided to send a great flood to cover the earth. I want you to build a huge boat. In this boat, I want you to carry your family and a pair of all living creatures, so that some may be saved."

Noah began to build the large boat which was called an ark. The strong sturdy ark was made of gopher wood. It had one window and one door. When the ark was finished, Noah gathered plenty of food. He needed to find enough food to feed his family and all the animals while they lived on the ark, because they would not see land for a long time.

Finally he was ready, and Noah opened the door. Noah's wife and family entered the ark, and then the animals came in two by two. There were creatures of all kinds.

Noah had never seen so many animals. The elephants did not look happy. "Don't worry," said Noah. "I have made the ark very large. There is plenty of room for everyone."

The birds fluttered in fear. "Don't worry," said Noah. "I have built the ark very high so you will be able to fly."

The lions roared in anger. "Don't worry," said Noah. "I have gathered lots of food. There will be plenty for everyone to eat."

After every animal was safely on the ark, they heard a loud rumble. It was the sound of thunder... and then the rain began to fall. The rain poured down for forty days and forty nights. Water covered the earth, and Noah's ark rose high on the water.

After a while, the animals became grumpy. The birds were tired of being chased by the lions. The lions were tired of being pecked by the birds. The giraffes were just plain tired. All the animals were bored and ready to run free again.

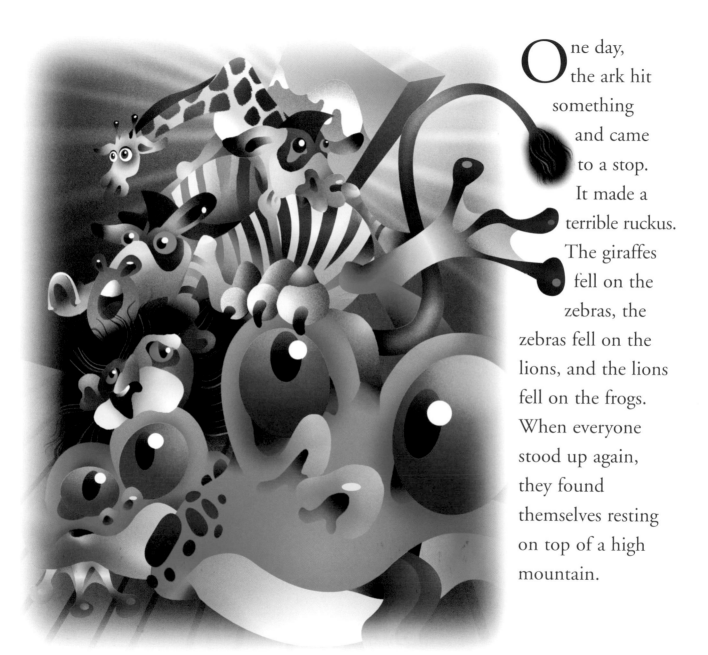

One day, the ark hit something and came to a stop. It made a terrible ruckus. The giraffes fell on the zebras, the zebras fell on the lions, and the lions fell on the frogs. When everyone stood up again, they found themselves resting on top of a high mountain.

Noah sent a dove away from the ark to see if the land was dry. When the dove came back, Noah knew the earth was still under water. Noah sent out the dove a second time, and this time it brought back an olive branch. This was a sign that the dove had found dry land.

Noah exclaimed, "Hooray! The earth is dry again. We can all get off the ark!" The animals were excited and could hardly wait for Noah to open the door. When the door was opened, the animals rushed outside. The birds flew high in the sky while the snakes slithered low in the fresh grass.

Noah said good-bye to the animals as they paraded off to find new homes. The elephants lumbered over the new land looking for food. The giraffes glided past in search of tall trees. The frogs hopped playfully toward the ponds. And every other living thing discovered a new place to live.

Noah and his family were happy with the work they had done for God. God spoke to Noah. "Noah," said God, "I am very pleased with your work, and I promise never to destroy the earth with water again. Look to the sky between the clouds for a sign of my promise and love." Noah looked up, and in the sky was the most beautiful thing he had ever seen. It was a rainbow full of bright colors.

So the next time it rains all day, and you think you will never go outside again, look for a rainbow. It is a sign of hope, and God's reminder that He will never destroy the earth by flood again.

I have set my rainbow in the clouds,
and it will be the sign of the covenant
between me and the earth. ...
Never again will the waters become
a flood to destroy all life.

—Genesis 9:13,15

JOSEPH
& His Coat of Many Colors

Adapted by Tess Fries

Once there was an old man named Jacob who had twelve sons. Of all his sons, he loved Joseph the most. Jacob gave Joseph a special coat of bright and beautiful colors.

Joseph's brothers were very jealous, for they knew Joseph was their father's favorite son.

Joseph had two strange dreams about golden sheaves of corn and sparkling stars bowing down before him. His dreams meant that one day he would be greater than his brothers. His brothers were so angry! How could Joseph think they would ever bow before him!

One day, Jacob asked Joseph to go and check on his brothers, who were many miles away taking care of their sheep and cattle. When Joseph's brothers saw him coming, they decided that they wanted to get rid of him, so that he would never rule over them.

R euben, the oldest brother, didn't really want to hurt Joseph. He told his brothers to throw Joseph into a pit (so he could rescue him later). Joseph's brothers tore off his colorful coat and threw him into a deep, dark pit. Joseph begged his brothers to let him out. He was so afraid!

A short time later, while Reuben was gone, some traveling merchants came by—and the brothers got another idea. The brothers pulled Joseph from the pit and sold him to the merchants for twenty pieces of silver.

When they got home, they showed their father Joseph's coat and told him that wild animals had killed Joseph. Jacob cried because he thought Joseph was dead.

The merchants took Joseph to Egypt. He looked at the towering pyramids and the great Nile River and wondered what would happen to him. Maybe he worried that God had forgotten about him. But God was always with Joseph.

Joseph was sold to a rich man named Potiphar. Potiphar liked Joseph because he was a hard worker. Joseph was cheerful and always told the truth.

One day, Potiphar had Joseph thrown into a prison. Potiphar thought Joseph had done something terrible, but he was innocent.

Joseph probably felt all alone in prison, but God was with him.

The butler and the baker for the Pharaoh of Egypt were in prison along with Joseph. One night they each had a scary dream. God helped Joseph tell them what their dreams meant.

Soon the butler went back to work for the Pharaoh. Two long years later, the Pharaoh had a strange dream. The butler remembered Joseph and thought he could help the Pharaoh understand his dream, so the Pharaoh sent for Joseph.

God helped Joseph explain the Pharaoh's dream. Joseph said, "God is showing you what He is going to do. For seven years there will be plenty of food for everyone. After that, there will be seven years with so little food that many people will starve." Joseph also told the Pharaoh how to save food now —so that there would be enough later.

The Pharaoh knew God had made Joseph wise, so he put Joseph in charge of his palace. When Joseph rode through the streets, all the people bowed before him.

Joseph forgave his brothers for what they had done and invited his family to come live with him.

God did not forget Joseph when he was scared and alone. He gave him courage and comfort and wisdom.

God knows everything that happens to you, and He will not forget you either.

*Now [Jacob] loved Joseph more than any
of his other sons, because he had been
born to him in his old age; and he made
a richly ornamented robe for him.*

—Genesis 37:3

MOSES
Baby in the Bulrushes

Adapted by Tess Fries

My name is Miriam. I am an Israelite who lived long ago in Egypt with my family. The ruler of Egypt was called Pharaoh. He made slaves of all of the Israelites.

We had to work very hard and quickly in the blazing sun. Some of us made bricks for the grand buildings in Egypt. Others planted and harvested Pharaoh's crops.

One day, my mother had a baby boy. We were so happy! We loved my brother very much. But Mother told me that Pharaoh had commanded, "Every son born will be thrown into the river, and every daughter will be saved." Pharaoh was afraid the boys would grow up to be strong men who would one day fight against him. My mother had to hide my brother from Pharaoh's soldiers.

As my brother grew, it became harder to hide him. One day, Mother made a sturdy basket from some bulrush leaves. She rubbed the outside of the basket with tar and mud so it would float on water.

Mother put the baby in the basket and took him to the river to hide him among the reeds at the bank of the river. The basket floated like a little boat, gently rocking in and around the plants near the water's edge.

I hid in the distance and watched to make sure my brother was safe. Suddenly, I heard people coming! I peeked out from my hiding spot and saw Pharaoh's beautiful daughter walking with her maids along the river. I held my breath and tried not to move. Then, the princess saw the little boat of leaves!

One of the maids picked up the basket and carried it to the princess. What would she do when she saw my brother? As Pharaoh's daughter opened the basket, my brother began to cry. The princess knew he was an Israelite. I could tell by the gentle look on her face that she felt sorry for him.

I stepped out from the reeds and asked the princess, "Would you like me to call a nurse to care for the child for you?" She told me to go find one, and I ran to get my mother. We brought my little brother home and took care of him for many happy months!

When he was still a little boy, my brother had to go to the palace to live with the princess. She named him Moses, and he became her son.

Moses grew strong and tall and lived like a royal prince in the palace. But he always knew he was an Israelite and was sad that his people were slaves.

One day, when Moses was a young man, he went out to the fields. There he saw an Egyptian soldier cruelly hitting a slave. Moses saw that no one was watching, so he killed the soldier. He hid the body in the sand and told no one what had happened.

The next day, Moses saw two Israelites fighting one another. He asked, "Why are you hurting your brother?" The Israelites were angry with Moses and said, "Who made you a prince and a judge over us? Are you going to kill us like you killed the Egyptian?" Then Moses was afraid that everyone knew he had killed the soldier.

When Pharaoh found out what Moses had done, he was very angry! Moses ran away into the desert.

He ran far away to the land of Midian. There he began a new life. He got married and became a shepherd.

Many years later, Moses was in the desert watching his sheep when he saw bright flames coming from a bush. As he walked closer, Moses saw that the fire was not burning the bush. He heard a voice speaking to him. It was God. God told Moses that with His help, Moses would rescue His people from their slavery and lead them out of Egypt!

My brother Moses never thought that God would ask him to do such an important job.

God has a special job for you, too. As you grow, He will let you know what it is and He will help you.

She named him Moses, saying,
"I drew him out of the water."

—Exodus 2:10b

NAOMI & RUTH

Adapted by Tess Fries

Long ago Ruth lived happily with her husband and his family in the land of Moab. Ruth's husband was from Bethlehem where they worshiped God. He taught Ruth about God, and she soon learned to love and worship the God of his people.

One day, Ruth's husband died. Her mother-in-law, Naomi, decided to go back to Bethlehem to her people. Ruth wanted to go with her. Naomi said, "No. You should return to your mother's house. May the LORD be as kind to you as you have been to me."

Ruth begged Naomi, "Do not make me leave you. Where you go, I will go. Where you live, I will live. Your people will be my people, and your God will be my God." Naomi saw how much Ruth loved her, so together they walked the many miles to Naomi's home. Over rugged hills and through valleys, on and on they walked.

Finally, they came to Bethlehem, but there was no one who could take care of them. People were working hard in the fields cutting the ripe barley. There was always some barley left behind in the fields for the poor to gather to eat. When Ruth heard about this she said to Naomi, "Let me go now and pick up the grain that is left behind."

Ruth began to work in the fields owned by a rich man named Boaz. When he came to the field he saw Ruth and asked, "Who is this young woman?" His servant said she was from Moab taking care of her mother-in-law, Naomi.

Boaz grew to love Ruth who was very patient and hard-working. He treated her kindly and told his servants to be sure to leave extra barley for her to gather.

During the harvest feast, Boaz said to Ruth, "May the LORD bless you, young woman. All the city knows that you are a good woman." Boaz married Ruth and took her to live in his beautiful home. They were very happy.

Because Ruth loved Naomi and was kind to her mother-in-law, God took care of Ruth.

May you be richly rewarded by the LORD,
*the God of Israel, under whose wings
you have come to take refuge.*

—Ruth 2:12b

DAVID & GOLIATH

Adapted by Tess Fries

Once there was a young shepherd boy named David. David was a happy boy, and he loved God very much. He wrote and sang many songs that told about God's power and His love for us.

One day, David's father asked him to deliver some dried corn and ten loaves of bread to his three older brothers. They were fighting in the army of King Saul.

David left the next morning. When he got to the army camp on the mountain, he ran to see his brothers. How excited he was!

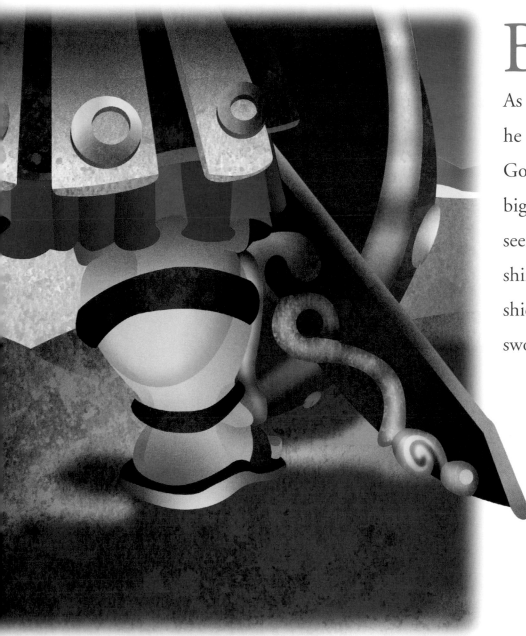

But the enemy's camp was right across the valley. As David ran to his brothers, he saw a giant man named Goliath. Goliath was the biggest man David had ever seen! He was covered with shiny armor and carried a shield, a spear, and a huge sword.

David's brothers told him that every morning and every night for forty days, Goliath had been shouting to them to send someone out to fight him. Goliath shouted, "If any of you can defeat me, your King's army will be the winner of the entire battle."

The King's soldiers were so afraid that they ran away each time they saw Goliath.

But young David was not afraid.

David went to the King and told him that he would fight Goliath! King Saul said, "You are much too small to fight this great giant." But David would not give up. He told the King that with God's help, he had defeated a fierce lion and a hungry bear who had stolen a lamb from his flock. David was sure that God would help him fight Goliath, too!

King Saul believed that God would help David, but insisted, "You must take my armor and sword to fight a giant such as Goliath." David tried on the armor and the sword, but it was too heavy for him. So he took only his staff and sling and went down to the river.

There at the river, David found five smooth stones and put them in his shepherd's bag.

Then David walked toward Goliath. Goliath laughed when he saw the boy coming down the mountain toward him.

David said, "I am not afraid! God will help me." Then he reached into his bag and pulled out one smooth stone.

David put a stone in his sling and hurled it toward Goliath. It hit the giant directly on the forehead. The giant fell to the ground with a thud!

When the enemy soldiers saw that their mighty giant had fallen, they all ran away in fear.

With God's help, David had won the battle for King Saul.

When you think you are too young and too small to help someone else, remember how God helped David defeat the giant. Nothing is ever impossible for God, if only you let Him help you!

Reaching into his bag and taking out
a stone, he slung it and struck the
Philistine on the forehead.

—1 Samuel 17:49a

QUEEN ESTHER

SAVES HER PEOPLE

Adapted by Tess Fries

My name is Esther, and I am a Jew. When I was young, I went to live with my cousin Mordecai. Mordecai worked in the King's palace. One day, he told me, "The King has decided to pick a new Queen. All the young maidens are to go to the palace. You must go, too." Mordecai told me not to tell anyone that I was a Jew. It would be our secret.

When I was brought before the King, he immediately placed the royal crown on my head. Great feasts were held in my honor, and all the kingdom knew I was chosen to be the new Queen.

I was happy
in the palace,
until one day
when my servant
brought a message
from Mordecai.
My cousin had
angered a prince
of the palace,
a proud man
named Haman,
by refusing to bow
down before him.
Mordecai believed
that men should
bow down only
to God.

This made Haman furious! He knew that Mordecai was a Jew, so he decided to punish all the Jews. Haman got the King to sign letters saying that all the Jews were to be killed. The letters were sent all over the country. Haman didn't know that I was a Jew and that I would have to be killed, too.

Mordecai told my servant, "Tell Esther to go to the King and plead for her people." When I heard this I was afraid. Anyone who went to the King without being asked would be killed unless the King held out his scepter to them.

But I knew I needed to help my people. So I put on my best royal robes and went to the King. Though he was surprised to see me, he smiled and held out his scepter. I was so thankful! I said, "Please, my King, would you and Haman come to a special banquet I have planned for you tomorrow night?"

When they arrived the next night, the King asked, "What would you have, Queen Esther? I will give you anything, even half of my kingdom!" I asked if they would come the following night for another banquet.

The next night I begged the King to save my life and the lives of my people. I told him that we were all going to be killed. The King was shocked! He said, "Who would do such a thing?" I told him that Haman was the man plotting against us.

The King promised that my people and I would be safe. He punished Haman and ordered that the Jews *not* be killed. I was so happy! In His wisdom, God had planned all along for me to be the Queen so that I could plead for my people and save them from harm. God knows everything—and nothing is beyond His power!

For the Jews it was a time
of happiness and joy, gladness and honor.

—Esther 8:16

DANIEL
in the Lions' Den

Adapted by Tess Fries

Daniel was a young boy who lived long ago in the city of Jerusalem.

One day, a great army came to Jerusalem and captured all of the people there. The soldiers took Daniel and many others far away to a strange land to work for their king.

Daniel was called to work in the royal palace. He worked very hard at all he was given to do.

Daniel had been taught at home about God, and he prayed to God every morning, noon, and night. He knew God was helping him do his work well.

Many years passed and Daniel continued to work in the palace. He was always honest and wise in what he did. The King grew to love Daniel. He put Daniel in charge of his kingdom, and Daniel never made any mistakes.

Other men working for the King were jealous of Daniel. They did not want him to rule over them, so they tried to catch him doing something wrong. But Daniel only did what was right. Daniel knew that his wisdom came from God, and he prayed faithfully to God three times every day.

The bad men knew they would have to trap Daniel into doing something wrong to get rid of him. So they went to the King and said, "O King, make it a law that for 30 days no one can ask anyone but you for help. Anyone who breaks the law will be thrown into the lions' den."

The King thought this was a wonderful idea. He didn't know the men were trying to trap Daniel.

Daniel heard about the new law, but he still went to his room to pray and to ask God to help him do what was right.

When the sneaky men saw Daniel praying, they ran to the King and said, "Daniel has been praying to his God instead of asking you for help. He must be thrown into the lions' den!"

How sad the King was! He didn't want to hurt Daniel. He tried for a long time to think of a way to save Daniel, but he couldn't change the law.

Finally, the King ordered Daniel to be thrown into the den with the hungry, roaring lions. He called to Daniel, "Your God, Whom you serve, will save you!"

Then the King walked slowly back to the palace. He was so upset he couldn't eat or sleep. He kept thinking of Daniel trapped with all those fierce lions.

Early the next morning, the King ran to the den and shouted, "Daniel, has your God saved you?" Daniel answered, "God sent an angel to close the lions' mouths. They have not hurt me."

This made the King very happy! He commanded that Daniel be taken out of the den and the bad men be thrown in with the lions instead.

Then the King made a new law that everyone in his kingdom should pray to Daniel's God because He saved Daniel from the terrible lions!

Three times every day Daniel prayed to God, and God gave him wisdom and courage to do what was right.

God will give you all that you need to do right, too. All you have to do is ask Him!

My God sent his angel,
and he shut the mouths of the lions.

—Daniel 6:22a

JONAH
& the
BIG FISH

Adapted by Tess Fries

Long ago there was a great city of Nineveh. The King and the people of Nineveh were very mean and did many things that made God unhappy. God decided to destroy the city. But He loved the people and wanted to give them a chance to change.

So God decided to send a man named Jonah to warn them that they must change. God told Jonah to go to Nineveh and tell all of the people of His plan.

But Jonah didn't obey. He ran to the sea and got on a ship that was sailing far away from Nineveh. Jonah thought he could run away from God.

But God knew where Jonah was and He sent a fierce storm that caused the sea to be rough and rolling. The sailors were afraid. They called on their gods to quiet the storm, but the winds blew harder and the waves grew higher.

They thought the boat would sink, so they threw some of the ship's load overboard. But that didn't help.

All of this time, Jonah had been sleeping in the bottom of the ship. The captain woke him up and said, "Get up and ask your God to save us—or we will drown!"

Jonah said to the terrified sailors, "Throw me overboard and the sea will become calm again. I am the cause of this storm." The sailors didn't want to throw Jonah into the sea. They rowed and rowed, trying to get the ship safely to shore, but the storm only got worse.

Finally, the sailors knew they must do as Jonah requested. They picked Jonah up and threw him into the furious sea. Immediately, the wind stopped blowing, the sea became calm, and the ship sailed away safely.

Jonah went deeper and deeper into the sea, but he didn't drown. God sent a huge fish to swallow Jonah whole. Jonah stayed in the belly of the fish for three days and nights.

Jonah was very frightened. He prayed to God from inside the fish. He was sorry he had disobeyed.

God listened to Jonah. He caused the fish to spit out Jonah onto the sandy beach. Then God told Jonah to go to the people of Nineveh and tell them what He had said.

The King of Nineveh heard Jonah's warnings and was afraid. He took off his royal robes and put on sackcloth and sat in ashes. He told his people to wear sackcloth and to tell God they were sorry.

The people of Nineveh agreed to obey God and do what was right from now on. And so, God did not punish the people of Nineveh. He loved them, and He knew that they were truly sorry and had chosen to do good.

Every day, you choose between right and wrong. God wants you to make the right choice. So remember, when a choice seems difficult, God will be there to help and guide you.

But the LORD provided a great fish
to swallow Jonah, and Jonah was inside
the fish three days and three nights.

—Jonah 1:17

The Birth of a
SAVIOR

Adapted by Tess Fries

The Roman ruler, Caesar Augustus, had commanded everyone to travel to the town where their family was from, in order to be counted. Men, women, and children of all ages went on their journey by donkeys, or shuffled slowly along the road.

Mary and Joseph were traveling, too. Joseph's family was from Bethlehem. He and Mary had to travel the long way there—even though Mary was going to have a baby very soon. No one could disobey the ruler's command.

Many months before this journey, the angel, Gabriel, had appeared to Mary with a special message from God.

Gabriel told Mary that through the Holy Spirit she would have a son and that his name would be Jesus. The angel said, "Jesus will be great, and his kingdom will last forever. He will be called the 'Son of God.'"

Now, as they traveled, Mary knew that it would soon be time for this remarkable baby to be born.

At last they arrived in Bethlehem. How good it would feel to stop and get a cool drink of water! Joseph went from inn to inn looking for one that had a room where he and Mary could rest, but every inn was full with the many travelers that had come to Bethlehem. Finally Joseph led Mary to a stable where she could lie down.

That night, in the dark and damp of the stable, the baby Jesus was born. Mary tenderly wrapped him in soft swaddling clothes and laid him in the manger.

Not far from the stable, shepherds were in a field watching their sheep during the night.

Suddenly an angel of the LORD came to them and a bright light shone all around them. The shepherds were afraid!

But the angel said, "Fear not, for I bring you tidings of great joy which shall be to all people. For unto you is born this day in the city of David a Savior, which is Christ the LORD. And you shall find the baby wrapped in swaddling clothes and lying in a manger."

All at once there were many angels singing, praising God and saying, "Glory to God in the highest—may there be peace on earth, and good will toward men."

When the beautiful singing was over and the angels went back to heaven, the shepherds said to one another, "Let us go to Bethlehem and see the child God has told us about!"

The shepherds left their flocks of sheep and hurried to the city. There, in the humble stable, they found Mary and Joseph. The baby Jesus was lying on straw in the manger.

The Savior had come—born in a simple stable.

Through his teachings and His sacrifice, He would give us eternal life—the greatest gift of all.

...and she gave birth to her firstborn, a son.
She wrapped him in cloths and placed him in a manger,
because there was no room for them in the inn.

—Luke 2:7